Saddam HUSSEIN

Dale Anderson

Lerner Publications Company
Minneapolis

To my wife, Mercedes, and my boys, Dan and Charlie, for their love, support, and help

Copyright © 2004 by Lerner Publications Company

This book is available in two editions:
Library binding by Lerner Publications Company,
 a division of Lerner Publishing Group
Soft cover by First Avenue Editions,
 an imprint of Lerner Publishing Group
241 First Avenue North
Minneapolis, MN 55401 U.S.A.

Website address: www.lernerbooks.com

Library of Congress Cataloging-in-Publication Data

Anderson, Dale, 1953–
    Saddam Hussein / by Dale Anderson.
        p.   cm. — (A&E biography)
    Summary: A biography of the powerful president of Iraq, Saddam Hussein,whose rule began in 1979 with a coup and the assassination of sixty-six men who were allegedly conspiring against him.
    Includes bibliographical references and index.
    ISBN: 0–8225–5005–9 (lib. bdg. : alk. paper)
    ISBN: 0–8225–9901–5 (pbk. : alk. paper)
    1. Hussein, Saddam, 1937– —Juvenile literature. 2. Presidents—Iraq —Biography—Juvenile literature. [1. Hussein, Saddam, 1937– 2. Presidents—Iraq.] I. Title. II. Biography (Lerner Publications Company)
DS79.66.H87 A815   2004
956.7044'092—dc21   2002013956

Manufactured in the United States of America
1 2 3 4 5 6 – JR – 09 08 07 06 05 04

CONTENTS

A

♠

SADDAM HUSAYN AL-TIKRITI
President

Following a U.S.-led war against Iraq in March and April 2003, the whereabouts of Saddam Hussein—shown here as the ace of spades in a card deck of wanted Iraqi leaders—remain unknown.

Chapter **ONE**

THE ACE OF SPADES

THE UNITED STATES, UNDER THE LEADERSHIP OF President George W. Bush, had a mission—to bring down the regime of President Saddam Hussein, Iraq's brutal dictator. For years, Hussein had been menacing Iraq's neighbors; stockpiling deadly weapons; torturing and murdering his own citizens; and, some people thought, aiding terrorist groups. Hussein refused to follow international laws. He didn't budge under economic pressure. His grip on power seemed ironclad.

After years of failed diplomacy and heated international debate, President Bush decided that there was only one way to get rid of Hussein: by force. On March 19, 2003, the president spoke to the American people. "My fellow citizens," he began, "at this hour, American and coalition [allied] forces are in the early stages of military operations to disarm Iraq, to free its people and to defend the world from grave danger. On my orders, coalition forces have begun striking selected targets of military importance to undermine Saddam Hussein's ability to wage war."

War had begun. Immediately, the United States unleashed its "shock and awe" campaign, a massive military assault designed to bring Iraq into quick submission. Day after day, U.S. bombs pounded Iraqi weapons factories, communications centers, military bases, airports, and other prime targets—including Saddam Hussein's homes and headquarters. Tanks rolled through the Iraqi desert. Artillery units launched relentless rocket attacks on enemy troops and targets.

The U.S. soldiers made the job look almost easy. Despite some early resistance, Iraqi defenses soon crumbled. Iraqi troops surrendered by the thousands. Within three weeks, the United States and its allies had taken the capital city of Baghdad. Thousands of Iraqi civilians, having suffered under Hussein's long reign of torture and murder, welcomed the Americans as liberators. With the help of an American tank, Iraqis toppled one of the many statues of Hussein that filled central Baghdad. When the statue fell to the ground and broke apart, many Iraqis danced for joy.

But it wasn't all over. The United States still had a lot of work to do in Iraq. It had to repair buildings, sewer lines, and power plants that had been damaged by the bombing. It had to restore peace and order to Iraqi cities. It had to set up a new government in Iraq—hopefully a democratic government that would give Iraqis freedom and a say in their own future. And there was one more job that President Bush and the Americans wanted to get done: They wanted to capture or kill Saddam Hussein himself.

It wouldn't be easy. Although many Iraqis had welcomed the American troops into Baghdad, other Iraqis remained loyal to Hussein. What's more, insiders reported that Hussein had built a network of bunkers underneath Baghdad, capable of withstanding even the most powerful bomb blasts. When American spies who were tracking Hussein spotted him on April 7, they knew they had to act quickly.

The spies believed they saw Hussein and his youngest son, Qussay, enter a popular restaurant in Baghdad. They immediately alerted military commanders, who contacted an already airborne B-1B bomber crew. Upon receiving their orders, the crew reprogrammed four two-thousand-pound satellite-guided bombs and flew in for a surprise strike. The attack destroyed the restaurant and surrounding homes and buildings. Had Hussein been killed? No one knew for sure.

In the following days, as U.S. troops searched the rubble for evidence of Hussein's remains, rumors began to surface that Hussein and his Qussay left the restaurant right before the bombs hit. Soon there were more rumors and reports that Hussein was still alive and well.

President Bush was not about to give up the hunt for his enemy, however. He wanted Hussein dead or alive. He also wanted Hussein's top ministers and commanders, as well as Qussay and Udday, Hussein's other son. Qussay led Iraq's internal security forces and was widely expected to succeed Saddam, while Udday—notorious for his flashy lifestyle and his brutal violence—ran television and news organizations. To assist in the manhunt, the military gave special decks of playing cards to all U.S. soldiers in Iraq. Each card was printed with a picture of a top Iraqi leader. The more important the leader, the higher the value of the card. Saddam Hussein's card, of course, was the ace of spades.

Who is Saddam Hussein and how did he come to be one of the most hated figures in recent history? How did such a person become his people's ruler? And why has he been so difficult to remove from power? The answers to these questions can be found in his life's story.

BRUTAL BEGINNINGS

Saddam Hussein was born into a poor Iraqi family on April 28, 1937. His father and mother were Hussein and Sabha al-Majid. As was customary in Iraq at the time, the father's first name, Hussein, became the son's last name. The name Saddam is an old-fashioned name used only by people of Iraq's lower classes. It has a harsh meaning, roughly translated as "a person who confronts" or "one who causes a collision that has bad results."

Saddam was born in al-Awja, a small village in north central Iraq, near the town of Tikrit. This part of Iraq has a violent history. A British official once remarked that Tikrit had an "ancient reputation for savagery and brutality." Saladin, a great general who lived in the 1100s, was said to have been born in Tikrit. In 1394 the conqueror Tamerlane built a hill there using the skulls of the enemies he had slain.

Al-Awja had an even worse reputation than Tikrit. The town name means "crooked," and its residents were thought to be violent and thieving. According to one Iraqi, when people from al-Awja came to Tikrit, "many merchants . . . shut their shops" out of fear that something bad would happen.

In this region, few people trusted each other. People counted on only their family and their tribe. Tribes consisted of many different families, all descended from a common ancestor. A person's tribe formed an important part of his or her identity. In fact, one's tribe was more important than one's nation, because for many centuries Iraq was not an independent country. It was part of large empires ruled from distant places. The ruling empires usually had little impact on people's daily lives. Rulers came and went, and Iraqis noticed little difference.

Tribes had a great effect on people's lives, however, especially in rural areas. Each tribe was led by a sheikh, a man who had authority and respect. When two members of a tribe quarreled over issues such as water rights, for instance, the sheikh settled the matter.

Saddam Hussein was born near Tikrit. Tikrit—like all Iraqi cities—was once decorated with huge posters glorifying him.

A STRUGGLE TO SURVIVE

When Saddam was growing up, life was harsh in Iraq. Many rural people faced grinding poverty. Homes were small and simple. They were made of mud baked in the hot summer sun, the same way homes had been made in that region for thousands of years. The typical home had only one room. There was no separate kitchen, dining room, or bedrooms.

One area of the room had a fireplace used to cook meals. Those meals were simple. People mostly ate bread, rice, and dates. Sometimes they managed to afford vegetables. Only rarely did people eat meat. Most families had no dishes or silverware. They simply sat around the pot where the meal had been cooked and ate with their hands, scooping mouthfuls from the pot.

When it was time to sleep, family members stretched

reed mats onto the mud floors of their homes. In most homes, the only other furniture was a chest or two to hold the family's few items of clothing. Saddam remembered that during his childhood very few people owned shoes. Those who did have shoes usually wore them only on special occasions.

There was no electricity in rural Iraq during this era. There were no radios or televisions. There was no running water, either. People bathed in the same ditches that were used to carry water to the crops. This water, which was usually dirty, was also used for cooking, drinking, and washing clothes. Poverty and poor sanitation led to disease. Illnesses like malaria and tapeworm struck many people. Around the time Saddam was born, nearly one in three rural Iraqi children died of disease before age one.

This was the world into which Saddam Hussein was born. His father, a peasant farmer, died around the time of Saddam's birth, though the exact circumstances of his death are unknown. Living in a fatherless home wasn't easy for the young boy. Other boys ridiculed him for not having a father. Some people say he carried a metal bar, which he used to fight other children.

His mother, Sabha, was a strong-willed woman. She often broke rules about how women should behave in Iraqi society. In Iraq at this time, women's lives were very restricted. They were not supposed to speak freely or travel without their husbands or another male relative. Yet Sabha walked in public alone, talked to men

Life in rural Iraq in the 1930s and 1940s was little changed from life in earlier centuries.

outside the family, and spoke out in family meetings.

But life for a widowed mother was difficult, and Sabha remarried when Saddam was very young. Her second husband, Hassan Ibrahim, was not an impressive man. In fact, his neighbors called him "Hassan the liar." After they married, Saddam's mother and stepfather had two more sons. Because they were Hassan's biological children, these boys enjoyed a higher rank in the family than Saddam did. Although he got along well with his half brothers, Saddam may have resented their favored status.

Hassan was a cruel stepfather, who was said to enjoy beating Saddam. According to some reports, he often said he wanted to be rid of the boy. Hassan did not allow Saddam to begin school along with other boys his age. Instead, when Saddam was about age six, Hassan made him work. Some accounts say he sold cigarettes or melons. Other stories say he stole eggs and chickens so that his family had food to eat. One official biography of Saddam says that as a boy he was "melancholy, lonely, and never young."

A NEW OPPORTUNITY

The closest thing Saddam had to a father was his mother's brother, Khairallah Talfah, a former army officer. In 1941 Khairallah had joined a movement to overthrow Iraq's king, who had backing from Great Britain. Khairallah and his affiliates wanted Iraq to be free of British control. For his part in the revolt, Khairallah was kicked out of the army and imprisoned for five years. By 1947 he was out of prison and teaching school in a village near Tikrit.

That year, Saddam's life changed dramatically. He left his mother's home and moved in with his uncle. He probably left with his mother's permission. The move might even have been her idea. She perhaps wanted to give Saddam some relief from his abusive stepfather. She might also have thought that living with his uncle would give Saddam a chance at an education.

Whatever the cause for the move, it meant that Saddam, then about ten years old, finally started school. Though he wanted to learn to read and write Arabic, the primary language of Iraq, school was not pleasant for him. Other children taunted him because he was so much older than the other beginning students. He often fought with children at school. Still, the school experience benefited Saddam. He was a quick learner with a sharp mind and a good memory. He stayed in school until age sixteen. During this time, he became close to his uncle's son and daughter, Adnan and Sajidah.

In 1955 Khairallah moved to Baghdad to take a new teaching job. Saddam moved with him and the rest of his family. Khairallah maintained his interest in politics. Despite spending five years in prison for his views, he still wanted to change Iraq's government. He and his friends discussed their unhappiness about Great Britain's power over Iraq's king. They spoke of their hope that someday Iraqis could shape their own destiny.

Hussein probably overheard this talk, and his own interest in politics grew. He became politically active himself. In 1952 many Iraqis rioted in Baghdad against British control of Iraq. Hussein, still a teenager, took part in those riots.

Around this time, Hussein's uncle introduced him to someone who would play an important role in his political life. His name was Ahmad Hassan al-Bakr. Al-Bakr was a cousin of Khairallah's and an army general who was also active in politics. Over time, Khairallah recommended that al-Bakr take young Hussein as his protégé, a sort of student or trainee. "Blood is thicker than ideology," Khairallah said in explaining his idea. In other words, Hussein was a relative of al-Bakr's, though a distant one, and a member of the same tribe. That meant he could be trusted more than a nonrelative who merely agreed with al-Bakr's political views.

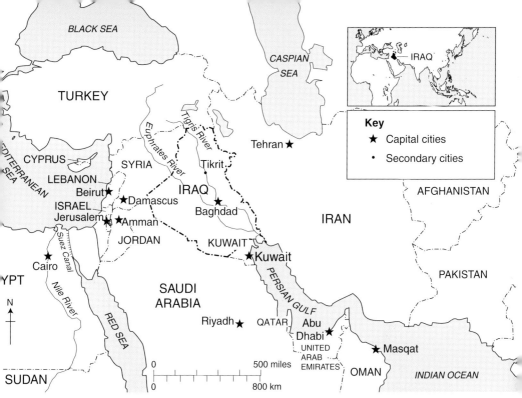

The borders of modern Middle Eastern countries were drawn after World War I and World War II.

Hussein hoped to become an officer in the army, like his uncle had been, and to gain an officer's stature and respect. In 1953 or 1954, he applied to the Baghdad Military Academy, where officers were trained. But he failed the entrance examination and was refused admission. This was a crushing blow to Hussein. The military academy was controlled by the British, and Hussein's family believed that he had been turned down because of his uncle's past political activity and his own role in the 1952 riots. Like his uncle, Hussein was growing to hate British control in Iraq. The refusal by the military academy only gave him one more reason to resent the British.

In a picture that probably dates from the late 1950s, Saddam Hussein appears to be a handsome young man.

Chapter **TWO**

THE FIGHT FOR INDEPENDENCE

IN THE MID-**1900**S, WHEN SADDAM HUSSEIN WAS growing up, new ideas were swirling through Iraq and other parts of the Arab world. For many centuries, Iraq and neighboring lands had been controlled by the Ottoman Empire, which was ruled by the Turks. Arabs had chafed for years under Ottoman rule.

The British fought the Ottomans during World War I (1914–1918), and many Arabs joined the British in this fight. When the war ended, the Ottoman Empire collapsed. Arabs hoped that Great Britain would reward them for their help in the war by granting them independence. Instead, European countries, especially Britain and France, took control of the former Ottoman Empire. Britain and France set up governments in

Faisal fought alongside the British against the Turks in World War I. The British made him king of Iraq after the war.

Syria, Iraq, Jordan, Palestine, Lebanon, Saudi Arabia, and other parts of the Arab world.

The British took control of Iraq in 1920, establishing a new government there. But Arab unrest convinced them that they did not want to rule the nation directly. They placed an Arab leader, King Faisal, in charge of the country. Faisal was dedicated to building a strong Iraq, but he also knew that he had to cooperate with the British.

When Faisal died in 1933, he was succeeded by his son Ghazi. The new king was only twenty-one years old. He was very popular with the people because he was anti-British, but he mostly wanted to have fun. He liked to fly airplanes and drive fast cars. He let other politicians run the country, but they were weak.

Late in 1936, an Iraqi general took control of the government in a military coup. The general hoped to rid the country of pro-British politicians. This action opened an era of instability in Iraq. Between 1937 and 1941, there were six more coups. The British managed to regain and maintain control through the 1940s. But among Iraqis, anti-European sentiment continued and grew stronger.

A DIVIDED COUNTRY

 ost people in the Arab world are Muslims, people who practice the Islamic faith. There are two major branches of the Islamic religion: Sunni and Shiite. These branches are bitter rivals. Most Iraqis are Shiite Muslims, yet when Great Britain set up Iraq's government in 1920, it put mostly Sunni Muslims in positions of power. This decision only deepened divisions between Sunnis and Shiites in Iraq. Unlike most of Iraq's people, Hussein and his family are Sunni Muslims.

Adding to the divisiveness, most people who live in the north and west of Iraq are Kurds, members of an ancient ethnic group. Like other people in the Arab world, the Kurds sought their own country after World War I. But instead of a Kurdish nation, Kurdish land became part of Iraq, Iran, and Turkey. The Kurds have not abandoned their desire for an independent homeland. They have revolted many times against their ruling governments, including Iraq's.

Thus Iraq is divided in many ways. King Faisal, just before he died in 1933, wrote a gloomy summary of conditions in his nation: "There is still—and I say this with a heart full of sorrow—no Iraqi people but unimaginable masses of human beings, devoid of any patriotic idea . . . connected by no common tie, giving ear to evil, prone to anarchy, and perpetually ready to rise against any government whatever."

UNITY, FREEDOM, AND SOCIALISM

This anti-European feeling grew not just in Iraq but throughout the Arab world. In 1941, a new political party, the Ba'ath Party, was formed in Syria. The party's three goals were revealed in its slogan: "Unity, Freedom, and Socialism."

As their first goal, the Ba'athists believed that the Arab world should be united—that Arabs from Iran in the east to Morocco in the west should live in a single Arab state. One Ba'ath founder, Michel Aflaq, envisioned "one Arab nation with an eternal mission." This idea was called pan-Arabism.

The next goal was freedom for the Arab people. The Ba'athists wanted their state to be ruled by Arabs, not Europeans. Under European control, Michel Aflaq said, Arabs were "a divided nation, a colonized and exploited one" that was "oppressed and enslaved."

The third goal was socialism, an economic system in which everyone shares in a nation's riches and enjoys a similar standard of living. In this system, the upper classes do not have excessive power, wealth, and privilege. The government, not private companies, controls major industries.

Finally, the Ba'athists hoped the Arab economy would grow strong, so that Arabs could become independent of European countries. These ideas appealed to many people across the Arab world. By the early 1950s, there were a few thousand Ba'ath Party members in Syria and small groups of Ba'athists in other countries.

A YOUNG ASSASSIN

Like many young Arabs of the time, Saddam Hussein embraced pan-Arabism. In the 1950s, he joined gangs of students who occasionally took to the streets to protest against the British-led government. In the process, he gained a new label, "he of the gun," a reference to a weapon he always carried.

A tall young man at six feet two inches, Hussein began recruiting young criminals and ruffians into his gang, ordering them to punish political opponents. For instance, his gang members beat up shopkeepers who refused to close their stores to join in anti-government protests. In 1956 or 1957 Hussein began attending Ba'ath Party meetings. He was only on the fringes of the party at first, but his gang and his gun gave him a reputation for toughness.

Many Iraqi leaders, such as General Abdel Karim Kassem, were unhappy about British control in Iraq.

In 1958 all the anger and bitterness in Iraq boiled over. A general named Abdel Karim Kassem marched his troops into Baghdad and seized the government. The British-backed king, regent, and prime minister were all killed, as were many other government officials. Kassem took over as Iraq's premier.

Iraq's Ba'ath Party supported Kassem at first. But the party quickly became disappointed with the new leader. Kassem showed no interest in pan-Arabism, a fact that angered the Ba'athists. In 1959 Ba'ath Party leaders hatched a plot to assassinate Kassem. They picked seven gunmen to carry out the attack. One of them was Hussein. His job was to provide covering fire for the other assassins.

The seven struck on October 7, 1959. As Kassem's car came by, the gunmen ran out and opened fire. Though they killed the driver, they only wounded Kassem. In the return fire, one gunman was killed, and Hussein was wounded in the leg.

In Hussein's official biographies, his escape is said to be heroic. His biographers claim that he used a knife to cut the bullet from his leg. They say the police followed him to Tikrit, where he swam across the cold Tigris River, borrowed a horse, and dashed to safety in Syria. In truth, his escape was less dramatic. A doctor treated Hussein's wound, which was minor. Hussein did go to Tikrit and then to Syria, but the heroic swim and daring ride across Iraq's countryside are fictitious.

Though the assassination attempt failed, it did achieve

something, at least for Hussein. In Syria he became a full member of the Ba'ath Party. In fact, Ba'ath founder Michel Aflaq himself gave Hussein this honor. Aflaq apparently took a liking to the young Iraqi tough.

TO EGYPT AND BACK

Since Kassem retained power in Iraq, Hussein had to leave the country for his own safety. For the next few years, he lived in exile in Cairo, Egypt. Gamal Abdel Nasser, Egypt's leader and a pan-Arabic hero, made his country a haven for pan-Arabic fighters from any nation. He gave them money to live on, though his police also kept a close eye on them. During his first two years in Egypt, Hussein finished his high school

This group portrait shows Hussein, front row, second right, *with other Iraqis living in exile in Egypt.*

Egypt's Gamal Abdel Nasser was a hero to the Arab masses.

studies, graduating in 1961. He began to study law at Cairo University, but he did little work and soon dropped out.

He spent a fair amount of time in the coffeehouses of Cairo. One coffeehouse owner remembered many years later: "He was a troublemaker. He would fight for any reason . . . We wanted to bar him from coming here. But the police . . . said he was protected by Nasser."

In Egypt, Hussein also made contact with agents of the U.S. Central Intelligence Agency (CIA). The American spy agency had a growing mistrust of Kassem because of his ties to the Soviet Union. These ties made him a threat to the United States, which was then engaged in the bitter cold war—a period of political and military hostility with the Soviets. The CIA wanted help in getting rid of Kassem. That's why they contacted Hussein, but the extent of the contact is unknown.

Meanwhile, back in Iraq, nearly sixty Ba'ath members were put on trial for the attempted assassination of Kassem. Seventeen were sentenced to death and executed. Hussein was found guilty and sentenced to death as well, but the sentence could not be carried out since he was in Egypt. His only chance of returning to Iraq was if a new government took power.

That chance came in 1963. In February of that year, the Ba'ath Party joined with some powerful army officers to overthrow Kassem. They brutally murdered him and removed his allies from power. They also launched bloody attacks on Kassem supporters, including communists, people who wanted a state-controlled economy with no private property. The attacks continued for months and resulted in a few thousand deaths.

With the Ba'athists in power, Hussein could return home. Soon after his arrival, he fulfilled a plan that his uncle had made years before. Khairallah had arranged for Hussein to marry his daughter, Hussein's cousin Sajidah. It was not unusual for an Iraqi to marry a first cousin. In fact, both husbands of Hussein's mother had been her cousins. A year later, Hussein and Sajidah had their first child, a boy named Udday.

Hussein and his party wanted to defeat General Abdel Rahman Aref, above, *who led Iraq in the late 1960s.*

Chapter **THREE**

GROWING
POWER

WHEN SADDAM HUSSEIN RETURNED TO IRAQ IN 1963, he was in his late twenties. He was not able to play a major role in the new Ba'ath government at first. He was still young and, having lived four years outside Iraq, had few political connections. Although he was only a minor member of the party, he had two valuable allies. One was Michel Aflaq, the party's founder and spiritual leader. Before returning to Iraq from Egypt, Hussein had stopped first in Damascus, Syria, and met with Aflaq. The Syrian talked a great deal to the young man, sending him home with his endorsement as a rising force in the party.

Hussein's other ally was Ahmad Hassan al-Bakr, the general who had taken Hussein under his wing as a

Ahmad Hassan al-Bakr, center, in uniform, *was the leader of the Ba'ath Party and an important power in Iraq in the 1960s and 1970s.*

young man. Al-Bakr was the prime minister in the new government. He was also highly regarded by the Ba'athists as their "father leader." Hussein had never been in the army himself, a fact that might have made his rise to power difficult. But being the protégé of an important army officer made it easier for Hussein to gain the respect of others.

HUSSEIN'S QUICK RISE AND THE BA'ATH'S QUICK FALL

On al-Bakr's recommendation, Hussein was given a job in the President's Bureau of the new government. The post was minor, but working in the office of the president gave Hussein a chance to look into any area of government he wanted to without being stopped. He became interested in a special police unit called the Bureau of Special Investigation. He also joined in with torturing the party's opponents, eager to kill anyone who stood in their way: "If there is a person then there is a problem; if there is no person there is no problem" was a favorite saying of his.

The Ba'ath Party soon found itself in trouble. Party leadership was split into three groups. One radical group wanted to make Iraq into a socialist state. Its leader was Ali Saleh al-Sa'adi. He organized a gang of violent followers into a militia called the National Guard. The second group was made of army officers who wanted Iraq to forge a union with Egypt and Syria in order to create a pan-Arabic state. The third group, which included al-Bakr, was more moderate than the others, although it tended to agree with the army officers. Tension among these factions grew intense throughout 1963. Hussein suggested several times to al-Bakr that he would be willing to kill al-Sa'adi to weaken the radical group. Al-Bakr turned him down but remembered the offer.

In late 1963, the conflict came to a head. The officers

Michel Aflaq, a Syrian Christian, was one of the founders of the Ba'ath Party and one of the party's chief intellectual leaders.

moved first, sending a group of gunmen into a party meeting. They captured al-Sa'adi and his followers, drove them to the airport, and put them on a plane to Spain. Hussein was the leader of the gunmen. The National Guard, al-Sa'adi's military backers, took to the streets in a wave of violent protests. Michel Aflaq came to Iraq to try to mend the party. He decided that the only solution was to exile the army officers as well. Suddenly, Iraq's Ba'ath Party was almost without leaders. Only moderates like al-Bakr were left.

The removal of so many Ba'ath leaders crippled the new government. It created a power vacuum. An officer named Abdel Salam Aref saw his chance. On November 18 he took control of the government. His troops hit the streets and quieted the National Guard. Soon after, the remaining moderate Ba'athists, including al-Bakr, were pushed out of the government. The Ba'ath no longer ruled Iraq—the army did.

Although Aref's seizure of power hurt the party, Hussein actually benefited from it. The loss of so many party leaders left openings for those who remained. Al-Bakr, Hussein's mentor, now controlled the party. In 1964 it was reorganized. Hussein's friends Aflaq and al-Bakr had him named secretary to the party's leadership council. Two years later, he was placed on that council itself. Meanwhile, Hussein worked to rebuild the party.

FAILURE, PRISON, AND ESCAPE

Hussein and the Ba'ath Party wanted to regain power. They put together two plots aimed at overthrowing Aref. First they recruited Aref's head guard, who agreed to allow Hussein to burst into a meeting and kill Aref. That plan collapsed when the guard was transferred to another post. When the second assassination plot was uncovered, Aref moved against the Ba'athists. Many party members, including al-Bakr, were arrested.

Hussein hid out in Baghdad, refusing to leave the country as some urged him to do. Soon, however, Aref's police located Hussein and surrounded his hiding place.

During the ensuing gun battle, Hussein ran out of ammunition. At that point, he surrendered to Aref's troops. He spent most of the next two years in prison.

According to Hussein's official biography, his life in prison was very brutal. But the evidence suggests otherwise. He was not tortured. He was allowed to read books and talk to the other prisoners. He later

Saddam Hussein, back row, second right, *shown here with fellow prisoners, was arrested in late 1964—little more than a year after his return from exile in Egypt.*

remembered that he "imposed upon himself a rigid discipline, rose early, worked hard, read much, and was one of the chief debaters in the prison commune." Hussein's reading material during this time included many books about Joseph Stalin, the dictator who ruled the Soviet Union from the 1930s to the 1950s. Hussein was fascinated by Stalin. He studied the dictator's methods in planning his own rise to power.

In prison, Hussein received regular visits from his wife, Sajidah. Through these visits, Hussein kept in touch with the outside world and secretly continued his party work. The method was simple. Notes were hidden in the clothing of his young son Udday, whom Sajidah brought when she visited. Another child joined the family during Hussein's stay in prison. A son named Qussay was born in 1966.

In July 1966, Hussein decided to escape from prison. It was surprisingly easy for him to do so. He and two other prisoners were being moved from one prison to another. They bribed the guards, who agreed to stop at a café. While the guards ate, Hussein and the other prisoners simply slipped out the back door into a car waiting for them. Hussein was free.

ANOTHER COUP

In April 1966, President Aref died in a helicopter crash. His brother, Abdel Rahman Aref, became the country's new leader. He was less popular than his brother had been and less capable. To maintain power, he needed

HUSSEIN AND STALIN

efore the 1968 coup, Saddam Hussein had made a promise to his Ba'ath colleagues: "When we take over the government," he said, "I'll turn this country into a Stalinist state." Stalinist governments, based on the practices of Soviet dictator Joseph Stalin, eliminate all opponents using violence, fear, and terrorism. Hussein studied and greatly admired Joseph Stalin. One Iraqi politician noted that Hussein had an entire library of books about Stalin in his office.

The two men had many things in common. Both had difficult childhoods in poor, rural areas. Both started their rise to power as the secretary of a radical party: Hussein's Ba'ath Party and Stalin's Communist Party. Both were tireless workers and excellent organizers. Both had sharp minds and iron wills. Both used their discipline and dedication to outmaneuver rivals. Finally, both were completely ruthless. Neither would flinch at eliminating anyone who stood in his way.

Stalin used several methods to ensure his grip on power. One was to purge all rivals. He used rigged trials and trumped-up charges as an excuse to murder potential opponents. He also created a powerful secret police that enforced his will throughout the country. Finally, he developed an effective propaganda machine—a system of spreading information and ideas—that celebrated his triumphs. During the course of his regime, Hussein put these same methods to use.

support, and he offered several times to bring Ba'ath Party leaders back into the government. They refused the chance to share power. They were biding their time until they could manage to take complete control of the country. Hussein spent two years doing the planning.

In 1967, Hussein and his party had a chance to weaken Aref's government. That year, war broke out between the Jewish state of Israel and several of its Arab neighbors. In just six days, Israel crushed the combined armies of Egypt, Syria, and Jordan. It seized the entire Sinai Peninsula and the Gaza Strip from Egypt, took the West Bank area (including East Jerusalem, a holy Islamic city) from Jordan, and grabbed the Golan Heights region from Syria. The Arab world was stunned. Iraqi crowds hit the streets to protest. They were angry that Israel had achieved such a complete victory and equally angry that Aref's government had sent only a small force to help the other Arab armies.

The Ba'ath took advantage of the unrest. Ba'ath demonstrators charged the government with being cowardly, corrupt, and incompetent. Protests continued into early 1968. In April of that year, Ba'ath leaders added to the pressure on Aref. They persuaded several retired army officers to issue a statement calling for a new government to be formed. They also made an alliance with four of Aref's current officers, who agreed to join in a coup. On July 17, 1968, the combined forces struck. The July Revolution was quick and bloodless. Aref was whisked off to a plane and flown to London.

Israeli soldiers in East Jerusalem. Iraq and other Arab countries consider Israel an enemy nation.

The Ba'ath Party set up a new government, led by a committee called the Revolutionary Command Council (RCC). Al-Bakr was made the committee's chairman, but Ba'ath members held only six of the twenty-four top posts in the new government. Non-Ba'ath army officers who had assisted with the coup also held considerable power.

Hussein did not have a high-level position in the new government, but he took a strategically important job. He became head of the government's security force—the secret police. Giving the organization the bland title of Office of General Relations, Hussein used the force as an instrument to increase his power. He also made another skillful move. He took the office right next door to al-Bakr's. From this post, he could carefully watch the chairman's comings and goings and step in when necessary.

TAKING POWER

The Ba'ath had needed the army officers to get rid of Aref. But it did not need these officers once Aref was gone. Ba'ath leaders had learned a key lesson from their loss of power in 1963: never share power with another person or group. Even before the coup, Hussein had told other party leaders what should be done to the officers. "They want to stab the Party in the back . . . ," he said. "We should collaborate with them but see that they are liquidated immediately during, or after the revolution. And I volunteer to carry out this task."

The first to be removed was Abdel Razaq al-Nayyef, former deputy chief of army intelligence and the prime minister in the new government. Al-Nayyef had been a key figure in the coup, but the loyalty he commanded among many army officers made him a threat. On July

30, he was invited to have lunch with al-Bakr. After he sat down, Hussein entered from his office next door, gun in hand, and informed al-Nayyef that he was through. Al-Nayyef pleaded for his life. Hussein assured him that as long as he cooperated, he would live. Hussein then packed al-Nayyef onto an airplane for Morocco.

Later that day, al-Bakr told the nation that the former prime minister had conspired with Iraq's enemies and was gone. Al-Bakr named himself prime minister and commander in chief of the army. That job was open, too, because another non-Ba'athist officer had also been ousted.

Hussein, al-Bakr, and their followers moved quickly. All remaining non-Ba'athist officers were replaced by loyal party members. The officers were not killed but were simply expelled from Iraq. Less than two weeks after using the army to help seize power, the Ba'athists were in complete control.

Near the top was Saddam Hussein. In the years since 1963, he had proven his worth to the party. He had also benefited from his uncle's support. Khairallah urged al-Bakr to give Hussein a high post in the new government, stressing the importance of family loyalty. Khairallah told al-Bakr: "Saddam is your son. Depend on him. You need the family to protect you, not an army or a party. Armies and parties change direction in this country."

Al-Bakr listened to this advice and named Hussein

deputy chair of the Revolutionary Command Council. That made Saddam Hussein, after al-Bakr, the second most powerful man in Iraq. He was only thirty-one years old. By then his family included three children. Sajidah had given birth to a daughter, Raghid, in 1967.

Oil became a mainstay of Iraq's economy in the 1970s. Above, workers labor on a pipeline to carry oil from Iraq's Kirkuk oil field through Syria to ports on the Mediterranean Sea.

Chapter **FOUR**

THE BA'ATH AT THE HELM

THE BA'ATH PARTY HAD RISEN FROM DEFEAT TO TAKE control of Iraq. Still, party leaders knew that their hold on power was uncertain. After all, Iraq had been scarred by several coups in the previous three decades. The leaders bitterly remembered their own loss of power in 1963. And numbers were not on their side. In 1968 the party had only about five thousand members, just a handful of people in a country of several million.

The first task for the Ba'athists, then, was to make sure that they stayed in power. That process had begun with the removal of al-Nayyef and the army officers who had helped the Ba'ath grab power in the first place. At first, the Ba'ath showed restraint. The officers were shipped out of the country rather than executed. But that early leniency soon gave way to bloodier actions, including kidnapping and murder. More death and terror were to follow.

THE STRONGMAN OF BAGHDAD

Ahmad Hassan al-Bakr, who held the titles of president, prime minister, commander in chief of the army, and chairman of the Revolutionary Command Council, actually did little of the work of governing Iraq. He left it all in Hussein's hands. Hussein became known as "the strongman of Baghdad"—the person who really wielded power in the country. He made the decisions; al-Bakr simply signed the papers and announced the results. But Hussein was careful to show respect for al-Bakr, who was highly regarded in the party and the country. He insisted on being photographed standing behind al-Bakr. He would not speak until al-Bakr finished speaking. He made sure that al-Bakr received public credit for every success that the regime enjoyed.

Behind the scenes, Hussein focused on removing potential rivals for power. Iraq's communists were considered dangerous for two reasons. First, they outnumbered the Ba'athists and were well organized. Second, they were popular among Kurds and Shiite Muslims, two of Iraq's most important groups. Thus the Ba'athists had political reasons for opposing the communists. What's more, punishing the communists would also give the Ba'athists some satisfying revenge. During Kassem's rule, communist gangs had roamed the streets and killed many Ba'athists. Now it was the communists' turn to suffer. Hussein's security organization arrested, tortured, and murdered hundreds of them. When the communists struck back by shooting at Hussein's house, his security forces killed a top communist leader.

Another target was Iraq's Jews. Jews had long been persecuted in Iraq. This persecution had become more severe after the 1948 creation of Israel, the Jewish state that was viewed as an enemy by the Arab world. Under the Ba'athist regime, a number of Iraqi Jews were arrested, accused of spying for Israel and the United States. In secret trials, they were found guilty and condemned to death. They were then hanged in public, with their bodies left on display as an example to others.

Former government officials were also hauled into court and convicted of crimes such as plotting to overthrow the government or spying. Some of the trials were televised, allowing ordinary Iraqis to see how their new rulers dealt with opponents.

All these actions helped solidify Ba'athist rule. Meanwhile, Hussein worked to increase his own power. His earliest steps were aimed at the army. First, he replaced all leading non-Ba'athist military officers with those whose loyalty could be trusted. Second, he placed members of his security organization in each army unit. Their job was simple: to keep their eyes on army commanders and to stop potential conspiracies. Third,

Hussein formed a well-trained, well-armed militia called the Popular Army, which he controlled. This step gave him an armed force that could be used to fight any army attempt to seize power. Finally, he removed all former army officers except al-Bakr from the government, replacing them with civilians. As a result, the military was no longer a threat. As Hussein contentedly told a journalist, "There is no chance for anyone who disagrees with us to jump on a couple of tanks and overthrow the government."

THE IRAQI PEOPLE REACT

The people of Iraq did not welcome the Ba'athists when they first took power. The new rulers, except for al-Bakr, were little known. More importantly, anyone who remembered Ba'athist rule in 1963 probably worried about what would happen next. In their first period in power, the Ba'athists had scarred Iraq with violent attacks on opponents.

The ruthless actions of Hussein and his security organization confirmed the people's fears. Iraqis became frightened and apprehensive. As one British journalist described: "[Iraq became] a place where men vanished, and their friends were too frightened to inquire what had happened to them; people [who were] arrested on trivial charges 'committed suicide' in prison; former officials were mysteriously assassinated; politicians disappeared."

One group that dared stand up to the government was

Mustafa Barzani led the Kurds in several revolts against Iraq's government, the first of which came in the 1930s.

the Kurds. Still seeking an independent homeland, the Kurds of northern Iraq had begun a revolt in the mid-1960s. They had begun to make headway against the Iraqi army. Their success was due in part to military aid, including troops, coming from Iran, Iraq's neighbor and frequent enemy.

The Ba'athist government was not yet strong enough to fight the Kurds, so it tried to make peace. Hussein met with a Kurdish leader, Mustafa Barzani, in 1970 and worked out a deal. In exchange for peace, he promised autonomy, or self-rule, in areas of Iraq where

Saddam Hussein, right, *is shown in a diplomatic moment during a conference in the mid-1970s with Reza Shah Pahlavi, ruler of Iran,* left, *and Algeria's president Houari Boumédienne,* center.

Kurds were the majority of the population. He also promised to give the Kurds a larger share of income from the sale of oil on Kurdish land. The final arrangements were to take place in four years.

But Hussein actually had no intention of taking these steps. He was just buying time. That became clear when the government took several hostile actions, including two attempts to assassinate the Kurdish leader. By 1974 the Kurds and the government were at war again. The government made some early advances, but aid from Iran once again helped the Kurds halt the army.

Hussein then made a diplomatic about-face that solved the problem. He signed an agreement with Iran's leader, Reza Shah Pahlavi. This treaty gave Iran access to the Shatt-al-Arab, a vital waterway along the Iran-Iraq border. In return, the shah dropped his support for the Kurds. The very next day, the Iranian army pulled out of northern Iraq. The Kurds were doomed. Within a month, the Iraqi army had crushed their revolt. From 100,000 to 200,000 Kurds fled the Iraqi army, becoming refugees. Their leader was forced into exile, and the movement for independence fell into chaos. It was a great victory for Hussein.

But there were more challenges to Hussein, this time from a close ally, Nazim Kazzar. Kazzar, second-in-command of Hussein's security forces, was known for his cruelty in torturing prisoners. He apparently decided that he and Hussein would clash one day and that he had the best chance of surviving if he struck first. So in 1973, Kazzar hatched a plot to kill al-Bakr and to make himself Iraq's leader.

Because of a delayed flight and miscommunication, Kazzar's plan had to be aborted. He raced to Iran to escape, but Hussein—who had learned of the plot—sent army helicopters and troops in hot pursuit. They caught up with the fleeing Kazzar and captured him. Soon after, he and more than thirty others were found guilty of conspiracy and executed. Hussein was shaken by the fact that this once-trusted aide had turned against him. He began to rely less on party members. From this point on, he placed his trust only in people from his family, his tribe, and his region. Various family members took high positions in Hussein's administration.

NATIONALIZING OIL

Iraq has great natural wealth in the form of oil—one of the world's most valuable fuels—but at the time, foreign companies owned most of the nation's oil fields and oil processing facilities. These companies paid fees to the Iraqi government for the right to pump and sell oil from Iraqi lands. The companies decided how much oil to pump and what price to charge for it.

Hussein and other leaders wanted Iraq's wealth for themselves. So in 1972, Iraq nationalized its oil industry. That is, it seized oil drilling and pumping facilities from foreign companies and gave the facilities to a newly formed Iraqi company, controlled by the government. From this point on, almost all income from oil sales went directly to the government.

Hussein was the mastermind behind this action, and it was very popular among Iraqis, who benefited from the wealth that oil sales brought to the nation. Iraqis were also pleased that business had been seized from foreign countries, long seen as oppressors of the Iraqi people. The Iraqi government radio station reported the news by joyfully proclaiming, "Arab oil for the Arabs."

Nationalizing oil gave Iraq not only monetary wealth but also political clout. That became clear a year later, when another war broke out between Israel and its Arab neighbors. Many Arabs were angry that Western nations, especially the United States, supported Israel during the war. In protest, Iraq and several other Arab nations reduced or stopped oil shipments to countries

The Arab oil embargo hurt the American economy. Gas stations could sell only a limited amount of gasoline each day and had to shut down when they reached that quota.

that aided Israel. As a result of the oil embargo, oil prices rose sharply in the United States and Europe. Prices stayed high even after the war in Israel was over. The result for Iraq was a windfall of income. In 1973, Iraq earned $1.8 billion from oil sales. By 1978, yearly oil sales were $23.6 billion.

THE ECONOMY BOOMS

Hussein and the Ba'athists used this newfound wealth to fund a variety of social and economic programs in Iraq. They wanted to improve life for Iraq's people. But their motives were not so much humanitarian as they were to ensure their own hold on power. Hussein knew that people were much less likely to rise up against him if they enjoyed a good standard of living under his

WOMEN IN IRAQ

Before the Ba'ath Party came to power, Iraqi women had few rights. Their fathers arranged their marriages. They were subservient to men in their families. They rarely attended school or held jobs outside the family farm.

The Ba'ath Party wanted to strengthen the role of government in Iraqi society and to reduce the power of the family. So the Ba'ath Party passed a number of laws that gave more rights to women, thereby decreasing control of fathers and families. Under these laws, women were allowed to marry and divorce according to their own wishes. They were ensured equal treatment in schools and workplaces. More women received an education than ever before, and more found work outside farming.

regime. "People with full bellies don't make revolutions," he explained.

The government carried out an impressive plan to modernize Iraq's economy and society. It invested in new industries such as iron, steel, and petrochemicals. It built or expanded roads, railroads, ports, and airports. It built schools and hired teachers, raising national literacy levels. It built hospitals and improved sanitation. As a result, fewer infants died of disease, and Iraqis began to live longer on average.

Iraq became a vibrant country, booming with construction and bustling with activity. People moved from the countryside to big cities such as Baghdad. The economic boom helped create a growing middle class. People were living more comfortable lives than ever before. In many ways, the Ba'athists brought great gains to the Iraqi people.

On the other hand, there was little freedom. The government tightly controlled newspapers and books. No opposition groups were allowed to voice their views. Teachers had to be members of the Ba'ath Party or at least agree with party positions. The party even controlled art. One university art department stated that its goal was to teach art "in the light of the ideas of the Arab Ba'ath Socialist Party." Free speech became virtually nonexistent. Hussein's security agents were everywhere, and people never knew whether or not they were being watched. It is little wonder, then, that one author titled his book about Iraq *Republic of Fear*.

Oil revenues led to a building boom in Iraq. Baghdad, right, *and other Iraqi cities began to take on a more modern appearance.*

ARMING THE COUNTRY

 addam Hussein was able to suppress internal revolts in part because he had such a strong army. In 1967, just before the Ba'athists took power, the army numbered only 82,000 men. Hussein launched a major military buildup. By the end of the 1970s, the number of soldiers had jumped to 242,000.

Hussein gave his new soldiers top-level equipment. From 1970 to 1975, the army doubled its number of tanks and armored personnel carriers. The number of fighter planes increased as well. The buildup continued late into the decade, when Hussein bought another 450 tanks, 40 more fighter planes, and 60 attack helicopters. This military buildup, like other government projects of the 1970s, was funded by Iraq's vast oil revenues.

In the mid-1970s, Hussein recruited more than four thousand scientists from around the world. They were given the task of creating chemical weapons, such as poison gas, and biological weapons —germs that could quickly kill large numbers of people. These kinds of weapons had been banned by the international community. But Hussein ignored the rules. His scientists produced supplies of several deadly gases and germs that caused terrible diseases such as cholera and typhoid fever.

Also in the mid-1970s, Iraq began construction of a nuclear power plant. Hussein publicly promised that he would use the plant only to generate electricity. But many nations worried that he would use it to make nuclear weapons, especially to fire on Israel. In the late 1970s, the new power plant was nearing completion. But several mysterious events delayed its progress. It has never been proved, but most experts believe that the Israeli government caused the disruptions. In 1981, just before the plant was to begin operating, Israeli jets bombed it and destroyed it completely. Nuclear fuel stored underground was not damaged, however, so Hussein's scientists still have a way to make dangerous nuclear weapons.

Hussein, whose troops are shown training, built up one of the largest armies in the region.

Guards stand before a portrait of Hussein in uniform at an Iraqi army base north of Basra.

Chapter FIVE

PRESIDENT HUSSEIN

FOR TEN YEARS, HUSSEIN WORKED CAUTIOUSLY AND patiently to secure the Ba'ath Party's hold on Iraq and to strengthen his own position. By the late 1970s, al-Bakr was growing old, and Hussein was entering his forties. His family included five children: sons Udday and Qussay and daughters Raghid, Rana, and Hala. Full of energy, Hussein bided his time, watching and waiting for his opportunity to make his final move for power.

The time came in 1978. Late that year, al-Bakr tried to engineer the unification of Iraq with Syria. By joining together, the two countries could put forward a stronger front against Israel, he said. Besides, both countries were ruled by Ba'ath organizations that had long called for the creation of one Arab nation.

Al-Bakr apparently hoped that achieving this unification would make him famous in Arab history. But his plan would not be good for Hussein. Al-Bakr planned to be the first ruler of the united countries and said that Syria's leader, Hafez al-Assad (one of Hussein's most hated rivals), would succeed him. The arrangement froze Hussein out. He could not oppose the plan, however, because it was widely popular. Many Arabs relished the idea of a pan-Arabic nation.

Fortunately for Hussein, al-Assad was not thrilled with the arrangement either and dragged his feet. By early 1979, the plan was losing momentum. To kill it completely, Hussein gave al-Assad an ultimatum: unify now or forget it. As Hussein expected, al-Assad refused, and the talk of unification was dropped.

The threat of losing power convinced Hussein that it was time for him formally to take control of Iraq. He prepared carefully. He made sure that the army was

Saddam Hussein and his family in the 1970s.
Clockwise from top left: *Qussay, Udday, wife Sajidah, Raghid, Rana, Saddam,* and *Hala.*

Al-Bakr (wearing hat) *greets Syria's leader, Hafez al-Assad, in Baghdad. Like al-Bakr and Hussein, al-Assad was a member of the Ba'ath Party, but he was also a regional rival, wary of an Iraq that was too powerful.*

loyal to him. He talked to the rulers of nearby countries and gained promises that they would not object. He then informed al-Bakr that he was taking over.

Al-Bakr knew not to resist Hussein. He agreed to put a nice face on Hussein's coup for the public. On July 16, 1979, he appeared on television to address the nation. Looking tired and worn, he said he was too ill to continue in office. He then praised Hussein as his worthy successor:

> During the bitter years of struggle prior to the revolution, Comrade Saddam Hussein was a brave and faithful struggler who enjoyed the respect and trust of the Party's strugglers. On the eve of the revolution, he was at the head of the brave men who stormed the bastions of dictatorship and reaction. During the revolution's march he was the brilliant leader who was able to confront all the difficulties and shoulder all the responsibilities.

With that, Hussein's mentor and protector of more than twenty-five years faded from view.

The new president moved swiftly to show who was boss. Less than a week after taking office, he staged a special meeting of a few hundred of the Ba'ath Party's top leaders. There, he forced some of them to admit to plotting against him, although in fact there had been no plot. Hussein read the names of the alleged conspirators, sixty-six in all. As he read each name, security police entered the room and took custody of that person. In a chilling scene, the remaining people in the room stood, cheering Hussein and demanding that the "traitors" be put to death.

The entire meeting was filmed, and copies of the film were distributed throughout the country so that all Iraqis could see it. Twenty-two alleged conspirators were sentenced to death, and Hussein ordered the remaining party leaders to join him in carrying out the executions. The men were shot in a basement room. Most of the rest of the alleged conspirators were thrown into prison.

MAN OF THE PEOPLE

What kind of man was the new president of Iraq? As his actions after replacing al-Bakr proved, he was ruthless. He was also smart. When he was preparing to nationalize Iraq's oil industry, the country's oil experts were astonished to learn how much he knew about oil production and economics. He was also a master at

A COMPLEX PERSON

t is widely known that Saddam Hussein is a cruel and ruthless tyrant, willing to kill anyone who dares to oppose him. One acquaintance said, "He never forgets an enemy. . . . He will go to extreme measures to get back at whoever [has hurt him]." Yet there is another side to him as well. Most remarkable is the story of an Iraqi Jew named Na'im Tawina.

In the early 1970s, Tawina was accused, falsely, of spying for Israel. He was thrown into an Iraqi prison. He had little hope for survival—a charge of spying usually meant death. One day, he was taken to a torture room. Just before the guards began to torture him, Hussein entered the room. He took one look at Tawina and said, "Do not touch this man. He is a good man. I know him. Let him go."

Tawina was relieved but shocked. He had no idea why Hussein had freed him. Years later, after he had left Iraq for Israel, he saw a photograph of Hussein as a child and finally understood why. Tawina had often bought cigarettes from that young child and tipped him generously. Hussein remembered his kindness and repaid the man with his life.

politics, finding clever ways of gaining political advantage over others. For instance, he correctly guessed that Syria's Hafez al-Assad's interest in uniting with Iraq was diminishing. He forced al-Assad to end the plan by giving him an ultimatum.

Hussein was tireless as well, working fourteen to

A mural of Hussein in traditional Arab dress dwarfs these young people at play in the streets of Baghdad. Murals and statues glorifying Hussein once abounded in Iraq, as part of Iraq's propaganda program.

sixteen hours a day. Hard work gave him a chance to become familiar with, and control, every detail of the government and the party. He also worked hard because he trusted few people other than himself. In a land where a close aide such as Nazim Kazzar could turn on him, or he could turn on al-Bakr, such mistrust was understandable. Hussein felt he could rely only on his family. Several family members held key posts in his government. His cousin Adnan Khairallah was the country's defense minister. A stepbrother headed one of three police organizations.

Soon after taking power, Hussein unleashed a propaganda campaign. Huge posters carrying his image appeared throughout the country. Often he was dressed in a suit, but he also appeared in a military uniform, in traditional Arab dress, or in Shiite dress, depending on what audience the portrait was aimed at. A joke made fun of the huge number of these posters. Iraq, people said, had 28 million people: 14 million men, women, and children, and 14 million pictures of Hussein.

Watches, plates, and calendars also carried his picture. Poets praised him as "the perfume of Iraq, its dates . . . its coast and waters, its sword, its shield, the eagle whose grandeur dazzles the heavens." In 1980 Hussein published his official biography: *Saddam Hussein: The Fighter, the Thinker, and the Man*, written by Amir Iskandar. It was full of praise for Hussein and packed with his own quotes.

Hussein also tried to cultivate favorable foreign attention. Party propagandists issued brochures and pamphlets singing his praises in Arabic, French, English, Japanese, Chinese, and other languages. Iraq even bought a glossy advertising insert in the *New York Times* that connected Hussein to famous Arab rulers of the past. It read:

Iraq was more than once the springboard for a new civilization in the Middle East and the question is now pertinently asked, with a leader like this man . . . will she repeat her former glories and the name of Saddam Hussein link up with that of Hammurabi, Ashurbanipal, al-Mansur and Harun al-Rashid [famous historic Arab leaders]?

Like most heads of state, Hussein and his family lived well. He built a series of bomb-resistant palaces, complete with swimming pools and impressive

A Closer Look at Islam

he Islamic religion, the major religion in Iraq and other parts of the Arab world, was founded on the Arabian Peninsula in the A.D. 600s by the prophet Muhammad. The Islamic God is called Allah. Muslims follow five basic practices called the Five Pillars of Islam. These practices are:

- Acknowledging that there is no God but Allah and that Muhammad is his messenger.

- Praying to Allah five times a day while facing the holy city of Mecca in Saudi Arabia.

- Giving alms, or charity, to the poor.

- Fasting from dawn to sunset during the month of Ramadan, the ninth month of the Islamic calendar.

- Making a pilgrimage to Mecca at least once in a lifetime.

kitchens. At the same time, Hussein promoted himself as "a man of the people." He made many public appearances, showing up at construction projects in a hard hat, at military bases in uniform, and even on a farm, where he wore a humble sheepskin vest. He tried to appear as a concerned leader. He sometimes slipped into crowds in disguise just to hear what people had to say. He even had his telephone number published so that people could call him with their problems and needs.

Although he himself was not religious, Hussein made a special effort to reach out to the Shiites, Iraq's religious majority. He proclaimed the birthday of an ancient Shiite hero as a national holiday. He also published a false genealogy, or family tree, that connected him to that hero.

WAR TO THE EAST

Hussein's friendliness with the Shiites was short-lived, however. They made up the majority not only in Iraq but also in neighboring Iran, which sits on Iraq's eastern border. In the 1970s, Iran had been ruled by Reza Shah Pahlavi. Like Hussein, the shah had tried to make his country into a modern industrial state. He also wanted Iran to be a secular, or nonreligious, society. This goal brought the shah into conflict with Iran's powerful Muslim leaders.

In a stunning turn of events, the people of Iran rose up against the shah in 1979 and threw him out of power. In his place arose Ruhollah Khomeini, a revered religious

Iran's Ayatollah Khomeini was a devout Muslim and a powerful speaker. His overthrow of Iran's shah sent shock waves through other Middle Eastern nations.

leader with the honorary title *ayatollah*, which means "reflection of God." Khomeini put in place a new, radical government controlled by religious leaders. He promised to remake Iranian society to reflect Islam's traditional beliefs.

Khomeini posed a double threat to Hussein. First, Iran was a powerful nation. The shah had built a large, well-equipped army, which Khomeini now controlled. Such an opponent could resist Hussein, who had plans to expand his own power in the region. Second, Hussein feared Khomeini's religious influence, and Hussein was not the only leader in the Middle East who felt this way. The ayatollah aimed to spread his radical religious message beyond Iran. Rulers in Saudi Arabia, Syria, Egypt, and other Islamic lands all worried that Khomeini's fiery words would lead their own people to revolt.

Hussein felt that threat even more acutely than the other leaders. Khomeini belonged to the Shiite branch of Islam. Shiites believed that Sunni Muslims such as

Hussein were not following the true path of Islam. Hussein feared that Khomeini would spur the Shiite majority in Iraq to revolt in order to create a purer Islamic state.

In fact, Hussein was right to feel threatened. For many years, the Shiites within Iraq had been a source of trouble for him. At one point, he kicked more than fifteen thousand of them out of Iraq, accusing them of having more loyalty to Iran than to their own country. Mohammad Bakr al-Sadr, an Iraqi Shiite leader, had welcomed Khomeini's rise to power and warned, "Other tyrants have yet to see their day of reckoning."

Hussein knew whom al-Sadr had in mind. His security forces arrested al-Sadr and his sister. Both were killed brutally. Afterward, Khomeini thundered in rage: "The people and army of Iraq must turn their backs on the Ba'athist regime and overthrow it . . . because this regime is . . . attacking Islam."

The two leaders hurled insults back and forth. Hussein declared that "Iraq is once again to face . . . the forces of darkness." Khomeini promised to send Hussein to "the trash heap of history." An aide to Khomeini called Hussein a butcher.

While exchanging heated words, Hussein was preparing for war. Iran, he reasoned, was weak. The new religious rulers had carried out bloody purges of the army and government, which would make it difficult for them to wage war. Khomeini, meanwhile, had been criticizing the United States and the Soviet

Union, making it unlikely that he would receive military help from either of them. The United States was especially angry because Iranian revolutionaries had seized the U.S. embassy in Iran in late 1979 and were holding a group of Americans hostage. No other Islamic state supported Khomeini either. All were afraid of him.

Hussein had much to gain in making war with Iran. If he were successful, he could count on the gratitude of other Muslim rulers. He could also weaken a force that threatened him both internally and externally. Finally, he could regain control of the Shatt-al-Arab, the waterway he had given up to Iran in the 1970s to quiet the Kurdish revolt. War seemed like a brilliant idea.

In late September 1980, Hussein appeared on Iraqi television. In his hand was the agreement that had given the Shatt-al-Arab to Iran. He tore it in half, proclaiming: "This Shatt shall again be, as it has been throughout history, Iraqi and Arab in name and reality, with all rights of full sovereignty over it." His action was, in effect, a declaration of war. Two days later, Iraqi planes bombed key points in Iran. Three days after that, the Iraqi infantry invaded Iran.

Hussein expected a quick, easy victory, and at first it seemed that he would get his wish. Iraq's troops advanced into Iranian territory and surrounded the vital oil depot at Abadan. They were unable to capture it, though, and revolutionary fervor soon led Iran to a spirited defense. The fighting settled down into a stalemate that lasted for more than a year.

In 1982 Iran launched a successful counterattack. Soon, Iraqi troops were being driven back, and casualties were mounting. By the middle of the year, 100,000 of Hussein's troops had been killed. Those still on the front lines had low morale and little desire to fight. The situation was so bleak that Iraq offered to withdraw completely if peace negotiations were started. But the Iranians pressed their offensive.

Hussein's war had become a nightmare. Some members of the government grumbled, but he was still in charge. In a meeting of cabinet ministers, the minister of health foolishly suggested that Hussein should temporarily step down. Hussein offered to "discuss the matter further" with the misguided minister in a room next door. After he and Hussein

Iraqi soldiers armed with rocket launchers and automatic rifles prepare to move against Iranian troops on the border near the Shatt-al-Arab.

entered that room, Hussein calmly shot the minister dead. Then he returned to continue his cabinet meeting.

Meanwhile, Iran had mined the waters of the Persian Gulf, a vital regional body of water, slowing the transportation of Iraqi oil by sea. At the same time, Syria's Hafez al-Assad, happy to have a chance to punish his rival Hussein, shut down the pipeline that allowed Iraq to pump its oil through Syria. As a result, Iraq's oil exports fell from 3.3 million barrels a day to less than 800,000. The resulting drop in income hurt Iraq's economy. Hussein cut spending, even reducing once-generous payments to the families of soldiers killed in the fighting. He borrowed money from other oil-rich Arab nations, including Saudi Arabia and Kuwait, and from European countries who opposed Iran.

In 1984 Hussein launched his own counterattack. Unable to count on his dispirited ground forces, he attacked Iran's oil tankers by air. If his enemy could not safely ship oil, he reasoned, other countries could not

The United States sent navy ships into the Persian Gulf to protect tankers from attack after the "Tanker War" broke out between Iran and Iraq.

buy it. The loss of income would hurt Iran's war effort. Iran retaliated by sinking tankers belonging to Kuwait and Saudi Arabia, nations assisting Iraq, creating a major international crisis. Finally, the United States sent ships to the region to ensure that oil tankers could safely pass. Meanwhile, the ground war once again settled into a bloody stalemate.

SHOWING HIS TRUE COLORS

Back in Iraq, Hussein faced more trouble from the Kurds. When they saw that his army was tied up fighting Iran, they revolted again. Fortunately for Hussein, the Kurds were split into two groups: the Kurdistan Democratic Party (KDP) and the Patriotic Union of Kurdistan (PUK). To quiet the Kurd rebellion, Hussein had about eight thousand members of the KDP arrested. At the same time, he made a deal with the PUK to give independence to the Kurds.

He had no intention of doing so, however, and soon the PUK leader realized it. He joined forces with the KDP. By 1985, Hussein's army, still embroiled with Iran, had to put down a major Kurdish revolt. Hussein responded harshly. He ordered the execution of the eight thousand or so prisoners taken earlier. He then placed a cousin in charge of ending the revolt. The cousin promised to "bury [the Kurds] with bulldozers." Army units entered Kurdish regions, rounding up about half a million civilians. Some were moved to prison camps. Males between twelve and fifty were separated

Kurdish fighters examine an unexploded canister of poison gas that was discovered after an Iraqi army attack on a Kurdish town in 1988.

from their families and executed in mass killings.

Hussein used the most lethal weapons available on the Kurds. On several occasions, his planes dropped canisters of poisonous gas on Kurdish towns and settlements. Thousands of civilians, including women, old people, and children, died in these attacks. In the worst attack, carried out against the town of Halabja in 1988, about five thousand people were killed and another ten thousand were hurt. The Kurds were forced to surrender. "The rebellion is over. We cannot fight chemical weapons with bare hands," one Kurdish leader said.

VICTORY AT LAST

The war with Iran continued, but by then morale in Iran was also ebbing, with fewer and fewer people volunteering for the army. In 1987 Hussein launched missile attacks against Iranian cities, including Tehran, Iran's capital. With military recruitment low, Iran could not respond in any forceful way, which made morale slip further.

Since 1982, some Iranian leaders had urged an end to the war. But Khomeini insisted on fighting until he could force Hussein out of power. In 1988, Hussein launched another punishing barrage of missiles and bombs against Iran's cities. He followed it with a new ground offensive, recapturing Iraqi land that had been

Hussein, left, *visited the front in late 1987, where he inspected the troops and received the assurances of his commanders that Iraq would triumph in its war with Iran.*

lost in earlier fighting. Khomeini finally gave in to the pleas of his aides and agreed to a cease-fire. It was, he said, "more deadly than drinking hemlock," a poison. In a radio address, Hussein proclaimed victory:

> Iran's leaders have to accept the peace road, they have to abandon their unjust dreams and foolish mottos and slogans, their hollow illusions after their defeats. Iraq stands now on victorious ground . . . confident today and in the future. Iraqis and the noble Arabs now stand on victorious peaks while the rulers of Iran are in the trench of defeat and shame.

But the victory had been costly. Estimates place the dead for both countries anywhere from 360,000 to 1 million and the wounded from 700,000 to 2 million. The financial cost of the war ranged from $600 billion to $1.19 trillion. Iraq's economy suffered during the war, and the government went deeply in debt. Oil prices fell, making it difficult for Hussein to restore the nation's economic health. The war had also embittered Iraq's people, especially the Kurds, who remained a threat to Hussein's regime.

Despite these costs, Hussein was satisfied with the results of the war. Khomeini had failed to oust him, as he had vowed to do. Hussein decided to celebrate his victory. He offered a $1.5 million prize to any architect who could re-create the Hanging Gardens of Babylon, a

Hussein's Victory Arch was the focal point of a celebration of his self-proclaimed victory in the Iran-Iraq War—a war that cost his country hundreds of thousands of dead and hundreds of billions of dollars.

structure that had been one of the glories of ancient Iraq. Another $3.2 million was spent renovating the palace of King Faisal, who was praised as an Iraqi hero.

Finally, Hussein built a Victory Arch in the center of Baghdad. The arch consisted of two gates flanked by sculptures of giant human arms. The arms, said to be modeled on Hussein's own, carried swords. The swords represented the ancient battle of al-Qadisiyah, where Arabs had defeated Persians, the early people of Iran, in A.D. 637. Steel nets draped over the gates' bases held thousands of helmets captured from Iranian soldiers. On August 8, 1989, Hussein dressed in ceremonial robes and climbed onto a white horse to lead his victorious troops on a parade beneath the monument.

An American soldier pauses in front of a portrait of Saddam Hussein, this one mounted in Kuwait City, during the Persian Gulf War of 1991.

Chapter **SIX**

WAR AGAIN

BY THE LATE 1980S, IRAQ WAS STAGGERING. IT had just fought a long and bitter war with Iran. Its economy was in a shambles. Industrial plants were not producing, and many cities needed to be rebuilt. The nation's debt was a mammoth $70 to $80 billion, and there was little prospect of repaying it. Oil prices were low, and many oil facilities had been damaged in the war. In the first year after the war, Iraq earned only $15 billion from selling oil, but it needed at least $10 billion more each year just to meet expenses.

Hussein tried to find help from other countries. Japan, which had lent Hussein money earlier, refused to lend Iraq any more. The Soviet Union began demanding payments for weapons it had shipped to Hussein years before. Desperate, Hussein looked to oil-rich Kuwait and Saudi Arabia, his neighbors to the south. Kuwait, though far smaller and less populous than Iraq, had oil reserves that were almost as large. Saudi Arabia had more oil than any single country. These states were fabulously wealthy, and Hussein wanted to get his hands on some of that wealth.

Making Demands

Both Kuwait and Saudi Arabia had been afraid of Ayatollah Khomeini's Islamic revolution. Both had given Hussein a great deal of money—as much as $40 billion in interest-free loans—to fight Khomeini. But Hussein argued that they had not done enough to help Iraq.

At a February 1990 meeting of several Arab countries, he demanded that Kuwait and Saudi Arabia forgive the loans they had made—that is, not ask for repayment. Then he asked for $30 billion more. "Let the [Persian] Gulf regimes know," he warned, "that if they did not give this money to me, I would know how to get it."

One source of his anger was that Kuwait had increased its own oil production after the Iran-Iraq War. This higher production level cut the demand for Iraqi oil and held prices down.

Hussein demanded that the other Arab states agree to raise oil prices. "War is fought with soldiers," he said, "but it is also done by economic means." Then he warned: "We have reached a point where we can no longer withstand pressure."

Meanwhile, other pressures were building on Iraq. The United States had issued a report that was highly critical of Hussein's torture, imprisonment, and murder of political opponents. The international community also worried that Hussein was trying to obtain nuclear weapons, especially in March 1990 when the British seized an Iraq-bound shipment of devices that could be used to trigger nuclear bombs.

In April officials in several countries intercepted shipments of parts that Iraq needed to build a "super gun." This big artillery piece would have been powerful enough to fire chemical weapons at any country in the Middle East.

Feeling increasingly threatened, Hussein stepped up the pressure on Kuwait. In mid-July, he accused Kuwait of stealing some of Iraq's oil and demanded $2.4 billion in payment. The next day Hussein warned, "If words

George H. W. Bush was president of the United States in the early 1990s, when U.S. reports critical of Hussein's regime were issued.

fail to afford us protection, then we will have no choice but to resort to effective action." A few days later, he sent thirty thousand soldiers to Iraq's border with Kuwait.

The crisis was growing worse. The U.S. ambassador to Iraq met with Hussein on July 25. She expressed concern about military action but reassured Hussein that the Americans understood his need for money. Some analysts say that Hussein may have viewed her response as an American "green light" to do whatever he wanted to do in Kuwait. Two days later, U.S. President George H. W. Bush sent a message to Hussein. He said that the United States wanted better relations with Iraq. He also urged the Iraqi leader not to use military force to settle the issue with Kuwait and emphasized that the United States would "support other friends in the region."

INVASION AND RESPONSE

By then, Hussein had nearly 100,000 troops on Kuwait's border. On July 31, 1990, representatives of Iraq and Kuwait met. The meeting broke up with no solution. That night, Hussein approved the invasion of Kuwait, and his troops marched in on August 2. They occupied the country in just a few hours. Iraqi soldiers began plundering homes and buildings, sending artwork and other riches back to their homeland.

But within days, what had been an easy military occupation turned sour. The world was not willing to accept Hussein controlling two huge sources of oil. The

United Nations Security Council quickly condemned Iraq's action and demanded that its troops be pulled back. A few days later, the Security Council put a strict embargo on trade with Iraq. That is, other countries agreed not to do business with Iraq. The embargo cut off Hussein's oil money, preventing him from buying more weapons.

The great fear in many Western countries was that Hussein would invade the kingdom of Saudi Arabia. Along with Kuwait, Saudi Arabia was the major supplier of oil to the Western world. If it were invaded, vital oil to the West would be cut off. Hussein's army was far larger than the Saudi army. On August 6, the king of Saudi Arabia invited U.S. troops into his country to help defend it. President Bush declared, "A line has been drawn in the sand." American troops were quickly dispatched to the kingdom in an operation called Desert Shield.

That same day, Hussein annexed Kuwait, declaring it was Iraq's nineteenth province. A few days later, though, he lost key support. A summit of Arab leaders condemned the invasion in a twelve-to-three vote. Hussein, growing worried, began to look for a way out of the mess he had created. He tried to split the Arab countries away from the United States. He hoped to win favor with other Arabs by proposing that Iraqi withdrawal from Kuwait be linked to Israeli withdrawal from disputed Arab lands. His hopes were dashed when even the Arab nations rejected this proposal.

American crews rushed to Saudi Arabia during Operation Desert Shield—the buildup to the Gulf War. They pose in front of missiles ready to be mounted on fighter aircraft.

Meanwhile, President Bush was forging a coalition of nations against Iraq. Some sent troops to Saudi Arabia. Some supplied the money needed to fund the war effort. Others simply supported the coalition diplomatically. Some nations opposed Hussein because they thought one country should not conquer another. Some feared his power. Some were rivals of Iraq and hoped to see Hussein weakened. Whatever the reason, Hussein was growing increasingly isolated. The number of troops opposing Hussein grew and grew. At one point, U.S. planes landed in Saudi Arabia every ten minutes to drop off troops or supplies.

Some efforts were made to achieve a diplomatic settlement. But the U.S.-led coalition insisted that any solution had to begin with Iraq withdrawing from Kuwait. Hussein created more ill will when he threatened to use Westerners—Americans and Europeans in Iraq on business—as "human shields." He threatened to position them at key military targets to prevent the Americans and their allies from bombing those targets. But the West stood firm, and Hussein backed off from his threat.

The noose tightened. On November 29, 1990, the UN Security Council approved a resolution that authorized nations to "use all necessary means" to expel Iraqi troops from Kuwait. The resolution also offered Hussein a final opportunity to avoid war. He had until January 15 to withdraw. But Hussein continued to talk tough. On December 31, he said, "Let them mass whatever numbers they can, because God will protect us from evil and save Iraq. To Bush's disappointment, the unprecedented U.S.-dominated buildup has failed to force Iraq to blink. . . . Iraq is growing more and more resolved not to cede any of its rights."

One major obstacle to starting a war still remained. The U.S. Congress had to vote to approve putting American troops in combat. There was some doubt that

Congress would agree. Iraq had the world's fourth largest army, and many Americans were concerned that war would lead to heavy American casualties.

Congress began debating the issue in January 1991. Some members wanted to wait and see if the trade embargo would force Hussein to back down. A CIA report, however, said the embargo was unlikely to have any effect. Meanwhile, on January 9, the U.S. secretary of state met with Iraq's foreign minister in a last effort to convince Iraq to pull out its troops. The meeting lasted nearly seven hours but produced no deal. Three days later, the U.S. Senate and House of Representatives approved the use of American troops to fight Iraq.

DESERT STORM

The U.S.-led effort to push Iraqi troops out of Kuwait, called Operation Desert Storm or the Persian Gulf War, began early in the morning of January 17, 1991. In the

Hussein's palaces, including the one at left, were among the targets of allied bombing during Operation Desert Storm.

first attack, American bombers destroyed Iraqi radar and communications facilities. The bombing continued for just over a month, with the United States and its allies attacking air force bases, missile sites, and Iraqi soldiers massed along the Saudi border. The allies also bombed Hussein's palaces, apparently hoping to catch him inside one of them. In response, the Iraqis fired missiles at cities in Israel and Saudi Arabia, inflicting minor damage.

Iraq's air force could not resist the overwhelming assault. In fact, Hussein had his military planes flown to Iran to wait out the war in safety. In all, the allies flew more than 100,000 missions and dropped 85,000 tons of bombs. President Bush and his commanders said that none of the targets were civilian, but at times bombs strayed or targets were poorly chosen. Iraqi civilians were definitely killed.

Hussein remained outwardly defiant. He told the Iraqi people that his army would triumph. "When the message of the Iraqi soldiers reaches the farthest corner of the world, the unjust will die and the 'God is Great' banner will flutter with great victory in the mother of all battles," he said. At the same time, he tried to convince the Soviets, formerly his allies, to work out a cease-fire. But no deal could be struck, and the bombing continued. Seeking some revenge, Hussein ordered his troops to set Kuwait's oil fields on fire and to release oil stored in tanks into the Persian Gulf. If he could not have Kuwait's oil, nobody would.

A tank, cars, and trucks litter the highway leading out of Kuwait City. The vehicles were abandoned by Iraqi soldiers fleeing the allied ground attack.

On February 24, the second stage of the war began. The United States and its allies unleashed their ground forces. In a carefully planned and overwhelming attack, their troops smashed into the Iraqis. Hussein's soldiers surrendered by the hundreds and thousands. Many more fled back to Iraq in retreat. Allied planes pummeled hundreds of vehicles jammed on the highway leading from Kuwait to Baghdad.

Toward the end of the Gulf War, Hussein ordered Iraqi soldiers to set Kuwaiti oil fields on fire. Workers at right labor to bring a new pipeline to one of these burning fields.

Soon, President Bush faced growing criticism, even from his allies, for the continued killing. Finally he announced a cease-fire to start on February 28. A few days later, Iraq's generals formally surrendered. The Persian Gulf War was over.

THE RULES OF THE GAME

The cease-fire agreement had several key elements. First, the United States and its allies declared that northern Iraq, where the Kurds lived, was a "no-fly zone." That is, Hussein's air force could not operate and threaten the Kurds in that part of the country. U.S. and British warplanes patrolled the skies over this region to enforce the policy. Later in 1991, another no-fly zone was created in Shiite territory in southern Iraq.

A second key part of the cease-fire agreement was a UN Security Council resolution concerning chemical, biological, and nuclear weapons. The United States and its allies feared that Hussein had gone quite a long way in developing these "weapons of mass destruction." As part of the cease-fire, the Security Council required that Hussein reveal all his research and production work on these kinds of weapons. The Security Council also created a body, the United Nations Special Commission (UNSCOM), to investigate Hussein's truthfulness about his weapons programs. The commission sent inspectors into Iraq to establish what the true situation was.

Third, the UN said that the trade embargo that had been imposed before the war would continue until Hussein complied with UN weapons inspectors. The embargo, also called sanctions, prevented Iraq from selling oil and importing food, medicine, and other goods. Western leaders reasoned that Hussein would cooperate and yield his dangerous weapons so that he could once more earn money by selling oil. They also thought he would not want to punish his people by denying them food and medicine.

Even with his defeat and the cease-fire programs in place, Hussein was not thoroughly beaten. Although his army had been badly mauled, its core remained intact. Most of the casualties had been Shiite and Kurdish recruits, whom Hussein was willing to lose. His most highly trained units, called the Republican Guard, were kept out of the worst of the fighting and escaped

WHY DID HE DO IT?

iven Hussein's overwhelming defeat in the Persian Gulf War, many people wonder why he made the decision to invade Kuwait at all. First, he never believed anyone would stop him. His talks with the American ambassador had convinced him that the United States would do nothing, even though President Bush had warned him against military action.

Second, once in Kuwait, Hussein had no easy way to get out. That was especially true when President Bush insisted on a complete Iraqi pullout. Had he withdrawn, he would have faced a bleak economic situation at home, aggravated by the trade embargo, plus the disappointment of his own people.

Even during the intense bombing, Hussein held out hope that he could win a ground war. He believed his troops would inflict heavy losses on the Americans, who would then give up. He told one aide, "Only we are willing to accept casualties; the Americans are not. The American people are weak. They would not accept the losses of large numbers of their soldiers." All of these assumptions proved wrong.

relatively unharmed. In addition, he still had the 800,000-man-strong Popular Army to enforce his will. He also gained a propaganda victory in the Arab world as the leader who had stood up to the powerful United States. Most important, he had survived. With his best-trained soldiers still intact, he kept his grip on power.

Saddam Hussein delivers a televised address to the Iraqi nation.

Chapter SEVEN

ON TOP OF THE RUBBLE

IN 1991 SADDAM HUSSEIN LOOKED WEAK. HE HAD led his country into two devastating wars. It seemed the world was against him. Certainly, the world's most powerful leader was. About a week before the Persian Gulf ground war had begun, President Bush had asked "the Iraqi military and the Iraqi people to take matters into their own hands and force Saddam Hussein, the dictator, to step aside." As Iraq's army retreated from Kuwait, Bush renewed his call for an Iraqi revolt.

Soon, Shiites in the south and Kurds in the north did just that. Hussein's days as a dictator seemed about to end. The Shiite revolt started on February 28, 1991, the same day the cease-fire began. It began in Basra, where a retreating Iraqi officer aimed his tank at a giant poster of Hussein and blew the picture to bits. Another officer described what happened: "We decided to put an end to Saddam and his regime. . . . Hundreds of retreating soldiers came to the city and joined the revolt; by the afternoon, there were thousands of us. Civilians supported us and demonstrations started."

While the Shiite rebellion spread, the Kurds in the north also rose in revolt. The two rival Kurdish parties joined together once more, hoping to finally win autonomy for the region. Within days, Kurdish forces captured important oil facilities at Kirkuk. By the middle of May, rebels in the north and south controlled about 60 percent of the country. Hussein was in trouble.

But the rebellion did not last. The Shiites pleaded for aid from the Americans. But their revolt raised American fears of another Islamic revolution, like the one that had occurred in Iran. The United States did not want a second radical Islamic country controlling oil in the Persian Gulf. After having called for a revolt, the Americans refused to help the rebels.

And Hussein knew it. His commanders intercepted a radio conversation between two Shiite leaders that revealed the American refusal to help. So Hussein confidently sent his troops to suppress the revolt. Using Republican Guard units, his generals recaptured one city after another in the south with bloody efficiency. Within days, the Shiite rebellion was over.

Then Hussein turned his attention to the Kurds. There, too, the result was swift. The Kurdish forces,

Kurdish refugees crowded the roads leading to safety in Iran after Hussein sent his troops into northern Iraq to suppress the post–Gulf War Kurdish revolt.

though more numerous and better organized than the Shiites, had only guns and other light weapons. They could not resist the army's tanks and artillery. They suffered heavy losses, perhaps as many as 100,000 people. Soon the fighters and their families escaped to mountain hideouts.

There was another reason, besides fear of radical Islam, that led the United States to back away from the revolt. Its Arab allies would not support replacing Hussein. Despite his misdeeds, he remained popular among the Arab masses. Any American-backed action to overthrow Hussein would probably have caused great unrest in Arab countries.

Sunni Muslims, too, backed Hussein, and they feared reprisals if the Shiites or Kurds were to come to power. So Iraq's Sunni Arab minority joined Hussein in crushing the Shiites in the south and the Kurds in the north.

In 1992, the opposition to Hussein rallied again, this time forming an organization called the Iraqi National Congress (INC). The United States helped fund the INC and openly supported it, partly because it succeeded in bringing together many different groups, including Shiites and Kurds. Still, the Americans did not believe that the INC was strong enough to overthrow Hussein. When the group attempted a revolt in the mid-1990s, the United States did not deliver any aid, and the uprising failed. Many top members were killed, and INC leader Ahmad Chalabi was forced to leave Iraq for his own safety.

PRESSURE FROM THE WEST

While opposition within Iraq continued to rise and fall, the United States and its allies put pressure on Hussein. The search for dangerous weapons, started by the UN

Special Commission after the Persian Gulf War, became a game of hide-and-seek. After the first UN inspectors reached Iraq, within a few months they were able to unearth evidence that Hussein had indeed been developing nuclear weapons. Hussein said he had told the inspectors everything about his weapons program, but further research produced more information. Over the next few years, the pattern continued. Hussein's people would claim they had shown the inspectors everything there was to show. Then UNSCOM inspectors would find something new. The Iraqi officials would then state that there was no more information. And UNSCOM would find something new again.

By 1994, UNSCOM believed it had gathered all the information there was. Then a top aide to Hussein, a cousin, defected from Iraq, leaving the country for his own safety. He had been in charge of a special weapons program, and he admitted that Iraq's work on chemical, biological, and nuclear weapons had been far more extensive than Hussein had revealed. Soon after, the Iraqis released about a million pages of new documents. They blamed the earlier concealment on the official who had defected, claiming he had done the research in secret. Nobody believed the story. The shocking news gave new life to the inspections. A few months later, Saddam lured the official back to Iraq, promising to forgive him. Instead he had the man killed.

Hussein then accused UN inspectors of spying on Iraq and demanded that they leave. For the next two years,

Vehicles carry UN weapons inspectors from their headquarters toward Baghdad's airport in late 1998. Hussein would not cooperate with the inspectors and made them leave the country.

Hussein managed to hold off inspections by first refusing them and then, in the face of American threats of force, agreeing to them. But before the inspections could take place, Hussein raised new objections. In 1998 he stopped any show of cooperation. While the United States continued to worry about his weapons of mass destruction, it could do nothing to stop him.

Tied to the weapons inspections were the sanctions—the embargo on trade with Iraq. The UN said that if Hussein complied with the inspections, Iraq could once again sell oil and other products and buy food and medicine from other nations. But rather than comply, Hussein let his people suffer. The sanctions devastated Iraq's economy. Prices soared, and wages dropped. The result was widespread hunger and disease. As the years wore on, the average lifespan for Iraqi men dropped by twenty years and for women by eleven years. A British journal estimated that by the late 1990s, 1.5 million Iraqis had died because of the sanctions.

According to one Iraqi officer who fled the country, the Iraqi people believed the situation was Hussein's fault. "Whenever he would start blaming the Americans for this and that, for everything, we would look at each other and roll our eyes," the officer said. On the other hand, the suffering of Iraq's people became a serious public relations problem for the United States and its allies. To much of the world, especially many Arabs, it was the West, not Hussein, that was killing the people of Iraq. As one Iraqi woman told a Western writer, "I will teach my children to hate Americans forever."

Concerned about its role in the suffering of the Iraqis, the United States joined other members of the United Nations in offering Iraq an "Oil for Food" deal. Under this plan, Hussein could sell oil as long as he used the income only to buy food and medicine for his people. Hussein delayed a year before accepting the plan. And even then, he undermined the program. Instead of distributing food to his people, Hussein's government sold it in other countries and used the money to buy weapons. Medical supplies were warehoused instead of shipped out to people who needed them.

In the early 2000s, the sanctions were still in effect, and Iraqis were still suffering. So the United States and Britain backed a new plan called "smart sanctions." Under the new plan, similar to Oil for Food, Iraq could buy food, medicine, and other goods used by civilians, although trade in military goods was still banned. It remained to be seen whether this new plan would actually benefit the Iraqi people.

"AN EVIL MAN"

As the suffering in Iraq continued, Hussein's police continued to suppress dissent. Lurking beneath the nation's surface was a deep fear of Hussein and his regime. As one cabdriver anxiously whispered to a Western visitor, "Believe me, ma'am, I am very afraid."

Hussein, meanwhile, lived a shadow life. Anyone taken to visit him was first placed in a car with darkened windows and driven around for hours so that he or she would have no idea of the destination. Visitors were searched to make sure they had no weapons or explosives. There were rules for how to behave when meeting Hussein. Visitors were told not to talk, just to listen. When Hussein entered a room, visitors had to rise and show him respect, but they were forbidden to approach or touch him. Meetings were videotaped.

The man who insisted on being called "hero-president" moved each night to a different secret resting place, where he grabbed just a few hours sleep. Three meals were prepared for him every day at each of his palaces, which numbered more than twenty by the early 2000s. That way, no one could know whether he was really at a palace or not. The food Hussein ate was tested for poison. In fact, the raw ingredients were x-rayed before meals were even prepared.

Meanwhile, American and British leaders continued to call Hussein a tyrant and said that he must be removed from power. The tension between Hussein and the West reached new heights after the September 11, 2001, terrorist attacks on the Pentagon in Washington, D.C., and on New York City's World Trade Center. Orchestrated by terrorists with links to the Middle East, the attacks focused renewed attention on the political problems facing that part of the world. Hussein blamed the United States itself for the attacks. He said the United States had inflicted great pain and suffering with its policies in the Middle East, such as the economic sanctions directed against Iraq, and was simply getting the payback it deserved. "The attacks on the Pentagon and the World Trade Center were the harvest of the United States evil policy," he said following the attacks.

Soon afterward, a new U.S. president, George W. Bush, the son of former U.S. president George H.W.

In the wake of the terrorist attacks on the Pentagon and the World Trade Center, President George W. Bush renewed the U.S. commitment to a hard-line approach in dealing with Hussein.

Bush, declared that Hussein was an "evil man" and that he must go. Early in 2002, Bush signed an order instructing the CIA to develop a plan to overthrow the Iraqi leader. But achieving that goal would be difficult. As INC leader Ahmad Chalabi said, "Saddam is a far better plotter than the CIA will ever be."

In April 2002, Hussein celebrated his sixty-fifth birthday. Baghdad was covered with his portraits. Television shows and newspapers proclaimed his greatness. Of course, all these praises came from Hussein's government, which controlled the press. But the message was also one of Arab defiance against the West, especially the United States and Israel. As one newspaper editorial said, "Celebrating our Leader's birthday is celebrating our resistance, resilience and rebirth. Saddam Hussein isn't president like the others, he is the symbol of resisting the [pro-Israeli] American plots to monopolize Arab resources."

In 2002 Hussein celebrated his sixty-fifth birthday—and his twenty-third year in power.

Is the Jig Up?

Saddam Hussein lived a life of luxury. He enjoyed swimming in his many palace pools, eating gourmet meals, and dressing in expensive silk suits. His friend Fidel Castro, Cuba's dictator, supplied him with fine cigars. Despite his defiance of the United States, he liked American books and movies. His favorite film was the American classic *The Godfather*. His children were all grown. He appeared to be grooming his youngest son, Qussay, to take over power in the future.

But Hussein's lush lifestyle was about to come crashing down around him. By the fall of 2002, President Bush was fed up with Hussein's evasion and deception, as well as the years of frustrating weapons inspections and economic sanctions that seemed to lead nowhere. The president began to rally the United Nations, international allies, the U.S. Congress, and the American people behind a plan to invade Iraq and remove Hussein from power.

The United Nations wanted to give weapons inspections one more chance, and inspectors returned to Iraq in November. As the inspectors were doing their work, President Bush continued his push for an invasion. Despite opposition from major allies such as France and Germany, the president and his aides felt that military force was the best solution to the Iraqi situation. As debates raged between pro- and antiwar groups in the United States and abroad, American leaders continued to accuse Hussein of supporting terrorism, stockpiling weapons of mass destruction, and terrorizing his own people.

By early March, several hundred thousand American troops were amassed at bases in the Middle East, awaiting orders from the president. On March 17, 2003, President Bush gave Hussein one last chance to avoid war. "All the decades of deceit and cruelty have now reached an end," the president said in a televised speech. "Saddam Hussein and his sons must leave Iraq within 48 hours. Their refusal to do so will result in military conflict, commenced at a time of our choosing."

In a statement issued by the Iraqi government, Hussein responded with his usual defiance. "Iraq does not choose its path on the orders of a foreigner and does not choose its leaders according to decrees from Washington . . . but through the will of the great Iraqi people," the statement read. "Any aggression against Iraq will make [the Americans] regret their tragic fate and mothers of the Americans who fight us will cry tears of blood."

Such words proved nearly hollow. After beginning their assault on March 19, American soldiers and their allies met with only minor resistance as they advanced through Iraq from the south and moved into Baghdad in early April. As they traveled, the American troops entered Hussein's opulent palaces, outfitted with priceless artwork and appointments, in stark contrast to the dire poverty of ordinary Iraqi villages. The soldiers also found evidence of Hussein's many atrocities,

U.S. general Tommy Franks walks through the rubble of one of Hussein's palaces following an air strike. Troops found no trace of Hussein himself.

including the mass graves of political prisoners he had had murdered.

The Iraqi regime quickly unraveled. From the American perspective, and the war appeared to be a great success. But where was Saddam Hussein? Neither American bombs nor American spies nor American soldiers had been able to root him out of hiding. He remained a slippery and tricky character. Perhaps Iraq's deputy prime minister, Tariq Aziz, summed it up best when he promised an American reporter, "You tell . . . General Franks [commander in chief of the U.S. forces] . . . that by the time he arrives here, he will be chasing shadows."

SOURCES

8   Office of the Press Secretary, "Operation Iraqi Freedom: President Bush Addresses the Nation," *The White House*, March 19, 2003, <http://www.whitehouse.gov/news/ releases/ 2003/03/20030319-17.html> (May 12, 2003).

9   Andrew Cockburn and Patrick Cockburn, *Out of the Ashes: The Resurrection of Saddam Hussein* (New York: HarperCollins, 1999), 11.

10   Said Aburish, *Saddam Hussein: The Politics of Revenge* (New York: Bloomsbury Publishing, 2000), 13.

14   Amir Iskandar, *Saddam Hussein: The Fighter, the Thinker, and the Man* (Paris: Hachette, 1980), 21, quoted in Aburish, *Saddam Hussein*, 17.

17   Aburish, *Saddam Hussein*, 23.

21   Samir al-Khalil, *Republic of Fear: The Inside Story of Saddam's Iraq* (New York: Pantheon Books, 1989), 160.

22   Sandra Mackey, *The Reckoning: Iraq and the Legacy of Saddam Hussein* (New York: Norton, 2002), 186.

22   Al-Khalil, *Republic of Fear*, 192.

26   Mackey, *The Reckoning*, 209.

31   Aburish, *Saddam Hussein*, 61.

35   Efraim Karsh and Inari Rautsi, *Saddam Hussein: A Political Biography* (New York: The Free Press, 1991), 26.

36   Aburish, *Saddam Hussein*, 67.

39   Karsh and Rautsi, *Saddam Hussein*, 30.

40   Aburish, *Saddam Hussein*, 79.

46   Karsh and Rautsi, *Saddam Hussein*, 49–50.

46   Ibid., 45.

50   Aburish, *Saddam Hussein*, 100.

52   Ibid., 98–99.

53   Phebe Marr, *The Modern History of Iraq* (Boulder, Colorado: Westview Press, 1985), 287.

59   Karsh and Rautsi, *Saddam Hussein*, 111.

61   "Gunning for Saddam," *Frontline*, 2001, <http://www.pbs.org/ wgbh/pages/frontline/ghows/gunning/ interviews/hamza.html> (June 3, 2002).

61   Karsh and Rautsi, *Saddam Hussein*, 39–40.

63   Mackey, *The Reckoning*, 257.

63–64   Ibid, 238–39.

67   Dilip Hiro, *Neighbors, Not Friends: Iraq and Iran after the Gulf Wars* (London: Routledge, 2001), 13.

67   Ibid., 15.

67   Mackey, *The Reckoning*, 250.

68   Ibid.

69   Ibid., 251.

69   Karsh and Rautsi, *Saddam Hussein*, 166.

71   Cockburn and Cockburn, *Out of the Ashes*, 144–45.

72   Mackey, *The Reckoning*, 263.

74   Ibid.

74   Julian Smith, ed., *The Rants, Raves, and Thoughts of Saddam Hussein* (Brooklyn: On Your Own Publications, 2002), 94.

78   Ibid., 204.

78   Ibid., 206.

79–80   Ibid., 212.

80   Dilip Hiro, *Desert Shield to Desert Storm: The Second Gulf War* (New York: Routledge, 1992), 94.

81   Ibid., 101.

83   U.S. News and World Report, *Triumph without Victory: The History of the Persian Gulf War* (New York: Times Books, 1993), 195–96.

85   Mackey, *The Reckoning*, 283.

89   Mark Bowden, "Tales of the Tyrant," *Atlantic Monthly*, May 2002.

91   Cockburn and Cockburn, *Out of the Ashes*, 13.

92   Ibid., 15.

97   Bowden, "Tales of the Tyrant."

97   Mackey, *The Reckoning*, 371.

98   Ibid., 305.

99   Smith, *The Rants, Raves, and Thoughts of Saddam Hussein*, 160.

100   Ibid., 186.

100   Bob Woodruff, "Happy Birthday, Saddam," *ABC News*, April 29, 2002, <http://www.abcnews.go.com/sections/world/DailyNews/ iraq_saddam020429.html> (July 17, 2002).

102   Office of the Press Secretary, "Iraq: Denial and Deception; President Says Saddam Hussein Must Leave Iraq Within 48 Hours," *The White House*, March 17, 2003, <http://www.whitehousegov/news/releases/2003/03/ 20030317-7.html> (May 12, 2003).

102–103   British Broadcasting Corporation, "Saddam Rejects Bush Ultimatum," *BBC News World Edition*, March 18, 2003, <http:// news.bbc.co.uk/2/hi/middle_east/ 2861029.stm> (May 12, 2003).

103   Public Broadcasting Service, "Waiting for War," *Online NewsHour*, March 19, 2003, <http://www.pbs.org/newshour/bb/middle_east/jan-june03/waiting_3-19.html> (May 12, 2003).

BIBLIOGRAPHY

BOOKS

Aburish, Said K. *Saddam Hussein: The Politics of Revenge*. New York: Bloomsbury Publishing, 2000.

Al-Khalil, Samir. *Republic of Fear: The Inside Story of Saddam's Iraq*. New York: Pantheon Books, 1989.

Cockburn, Andrew, and Patrick Cockburn. *Out of the Ashes: The Resurrection of Saddam Hussein*. New York: HarperCollins, 1999.

Hiro, Dilip. *Desert Shield to Desert Storm: The Second Gulf War*. New York: Routledge, 1992.

———. *Neighbors, Not Friends: Iraq and Iran after the Gulf Wars*. London: Routledge, 2001.

Karsh, Efraim, and Inari Rautsi. *Saddam Hussein: A Political Biography*. New York: The Free Press, 1991.

Mackey, Sandra. *The Reckoning: Iraq and the Legacy of Saddam Hussein*. New York: Norton, 2002.

Marr, Phebe. *The Modern History of Iraq*. Boulder, Colorado: Westview Press, 1985.

Smith, Julian, ed. *The Rants, Raves, and Thoughts of Saddam Hussein*. Brooklyn: On Your Own Publications, 2002.

U.S. News and World Report. *Triumph without Victory: The History of the Persian Gulf War*. New York: Times Books, 1993.

WEBSITES

Butt, Gerald. "Saddam Hussein Profile." *BBC News*. January 4, 2001. <http://:news.bbc.co.uk/hi/english/world/middle_east/newsid_1100000/110 0529.stm> (June 3, 2002).

Hafidh, Hassan. "Defiant Speech," *ABC News*. n.d. <www.abcnews.go.com/sections/world/DailyNews/saddam021717_speech. html> (July 17, 2002).

Kafala, Tarik. "Analysis: After Saddam Hussein." *BBC News*. March 19, 2002. <http://news.bbc.co.uk/hi/English/world/middle_east/newsid_1879000/187 9841.stm> (June 3, 2002).

"No-Fly Zones: The Legal Position." *BBC News*. February 19, 2001. <http://news.bbc.co.uk/hi/English/world/middle_east/newsid_1175000/117 5950.stm> (June 3, 2002).

"Who's Who in the Iraqi Opposition." *BBC News*. March 21, 2002. <http://news.bbc.co.uk/hi/english/world/middle_east/newsid_18810000/18 81381.stm> (June 3, 2002).

FOR FURTHER READING

BOOKS

Armstrong, Karen. *Islam: A Short History*. New York: Modern Library, 2000.

Bengio, Ofra, ed. *Saddam Speaks on the Gulf Crisis: A Collection of Documents*. Tel Aviv, Israel: Tel Aviv University, 1992.

Clark, Charles. *Islam*. San Diego: Greenhaven Press, 2002.

Egendorf, Laura. *Terrorism: Opposing Viewpoints*. San Diego: Greenhaven Press, 2000.

Harris, Nathaniel. *Israel and the Arab Nations in Conflict*. Austin, TX: Raintree/Steck-Vaughn, 1999.

Kort, Michael. *The Handbook of the Middle East*. Brookfield, CT: Twenty-First Century Books, 2002.

Lewis, Bernard. *The Middle East: A Brief History of the Last 2,000 Years*. New York: Touchstone Books, 1997.

Lo Baido, Anthony. *The Kurds of Asia*. Minneapolis: Lerner Publications Company, 2003.

Makiya, Kanan. *Cruelty and Silence: War, Tyranny, Uprising, and the Arab World*. New York: Norton, 1993.

Nardo, Don. *The War Against Iraq*. San Diego: Lucent Books, 2001.

Service, Pamela F. *Mesopotamia*. Tarrytown, NY: Marshall Cavendish, 1999.

Spencer, William. *Iraq: Old Land, New Nation in Conflict*. Brookfield, CT: Twenty-First Century Books, 2000.

Taus-Bolstad, Stacy. *Iran in Pictures*. Minneapolis: Lerner Publications Company, 2004.

———. *Iraq in Pictures*. Minneapolis: Lerner Publications Company, 2004.

WEBSITES

"Gunning for Saddam." *Frontline*.
<http://www.pbs.org/wgbh/pages/frontline/shows/gunning>

"Iraq." *CIA World Factbook*.
<http://www.odci.gov/cia/publications/factbook/geos/iz.html>

"Saddam Hussein's Iraq." *U.S. Department of State, International Information Programs*.
<http://www.usinfo.state.gov/regional/nea/iraq/iraq99.htm>

"The Survival of Saddam." *Frontline*.
<http://www.pbs.org/wgbh/pages/frontline/shows/saddam>

GLOSSARY

Arabs: people who speak the Arabic language. Most Arabs practice the Islamic religion and live in the Middle East and North Africa.

autonomy: self-governance for a group of people

coalition: a temporary alliance formed by two or more countries to achieve a common goal

communists: people who favor a state-controlled economy, with property owned by the community rather than private individuals

coup: a sudden seizure of governmental power, often by military force

defect: to leave one's nation, usually because of political differences with the government. Also to leave one group or political party to join another.

embargo: a prohibition on trade with a particular country

exile: a forced absence from one's home country

Islam: a religion founded on the Arabian peninsula by the prophet Muhammad in the A.D. 600s that is practiced by the majority of people in the Middle East and North Africa

Kurds: an ancient ethnic group based in Iraq, Turkey, and Iran

Muslim: a person who practices the Islamic faith

nationalize: to take over property owned by private companies and turn it over to the government

nuclear weapons: weapons that derive their power from nuclear reactions. Nuclear weapons are more deadly and destructive than conventional bombs.

propaganda: slanted or biased information or artwork aimed at persuading people to think in a certain way. Dictators often use propaganda to win the support of their people.

purge: to force opponents or critics out of a government or party by imprisoning, executing, or exiling them

sanctions: military or economic measures aimed at forcing a nation to cooperate with international law

sheikh: the leader of an Arab tribe. Sheikhs are responsible for defense of their tribes and settling disputes among tribe members.

Shiite Muslims: members of one of the two major branches of Islam. Members of the other branch are called Sunni Muslims.

socialism: an economic system in which all people share a similar standard of living, and major industries are controlled by the government, not by private companies

Sunni Muslims: members of one of the two major branches of Islam. Members of the other branch are called Shiite Muslims.

tribe: a large group of families, generally descended from a common ancestor

the West: the nations of Western Europe and North America

INDEX

OTHER TITLES FROM LERNER AND A&E®:

Arthur Ashe
The Beatles
Benjamin Franklin
Bill Gates
Bruce Lee
Carl Sagan
Chief Crazy Horse
Christopher Reeve
Colin Powell
Daring Pirate Women
Edgar Allan Poe
Eleanor Roosevelt
George W. Bush
George Lucas
Gloria Estefan
Jack London
Jacques Cousteau
Jane Austen
Jesse Owens
Jesse Ventura
Jimi Hendrix
John Glenn
Latin Sensations
Legends of Dracula

Legends of Santa Claus
Louisa May Alcott
Madeleine Albright
Malcolm X
Mark Twain
Maya Angelou
Mohandas Gandhi
Mother Teresa
Nelson Mandela
Oprah Winfrey
Osama bin Laden
Princess Diana
Queen Cleopatra
Queen Elizabeth I
Queen Latifah
Rosie O'Donnell
Saint Joan of Arc
Thurgood Marshall
Tiger Woods
William Shakespeare
Wilma Rudolph
Women in Space
Women of the Wild West
Yasser Arafat

ABOUT THE AUTHOR

Dale Anderson studied literature and history at Harvard University. He is the author of several books of history for young people. He lives in Pennsylvania with his wife and two sons.

PHOTO ACKNOWLEDGMENTS

Photographs used with the permission of: Popperfoto, pp. 2, 12, 14, 23, 26, 28, 51, 53, 62 (Yannis Behrakis), 79 (J. D. Ake), 86; © Todd Strand/Independent Picture Service, p. 6; Katz/Gamma, pp. 18, 25, 34, 55, 58; Camera Press, pp. 20, 47 (Lord Kilbracken), 56, 59, 75 (Allan McCullough), 82; Topham Picturepoint, pp. 30, 84, 87; Popperfoto/Reuters, pp. 32, 90 (Iraqi TV), 96; Corbis, pp. 38, 42, 48, 72; Rex Features/Sipa, pp. 66 (Michel Setboun), 70 (DeMulder), 73 (Kol Al Arab), 93 (Mohammad Farnood), 99, 100; Popperfoto/UPI, p. 69; Topham/Image Works, p. 76; United States Department of Defense photo by Sgt. 1st Class David K. Dismukes, p. 103.

Cover photos (hard cover and soft cover): front, © Pier Cavendish/ZUMA Press; back, Gamma Presse Images/Gamma Press USA, Inc.

WEBSITES

The website addresses (URLs) included in this book were valid at the time of printing. However, because of the nature of the Internet, it is possible that some addresses may have changed, or sites may have changed or closed down since publication. While the author, packager, and publisher regret any inconvenience this may cause readers, no responsibility for any such changes can be accepted by the author, packager, or publisher.